SLAB, COIL, and PINCH

A BEGINNER'S POTTERY BOOK

BY ALICE GILBREATH

illustrated by Barbara Fiore

William Morrow and Company
New York 1977

Library of Congress Cataloging in Publication Data

Gilbreath, Alice Thompson.
  Slab, coil, and pinch.

  SUMMARY: Twelve different projects with complete directions introduce the three basic types of hand-built pottery.
  1. Pottery craft—Juvenile literature. [1. Pottery craft. 2. Handicraft]
I. Fiore, Barbara. II. Title.
TT921.G54   738.1′4   76-48742
ISBN 0-688-22105-X
ISBN 0-688-32105-4 lib. bdg.

I gratefully acknowledge the help and advice of my pottery teacher and friend, Virginia Sweet.

CONTENTS

To our newest daughter,
Sue,
with much love.

A TIMELESS CRAFT

Thousands of years ago, someone discovered that a mixture of clay and water could be molded by hand into a dish or pot that would keep its shape after the clay dried. The container could then be used to hold or store food. And so the craft of pottery making began.

At first the pottery was rough and bumpy and was simply left in the sun to dry. Then, perhaps by accident, it was discovered that fire would make the pottery stronger, so pots were baked in open fires and later in crude ovens. People began making pots in different shapes and sizes, scratching designs on them, and experimenting with colors.

Different civilizations developed different kinds of pottery. We know the Egyptians made handsome glazed pottery as early as 3000 B.C. The American Indians were making pottery long before the first European settlers arrived. And by the 1700s, sturdy pottery was being made by the colonists at home and in small commercial potteries. As the demand for pottery increased, so did the number of potteries. Today we can choose from a large variety of attractive pottery pieces from all over the world.

Pottery making is a creative hobby for people of all ages. It can be very simple or highly complex, depending on the potter's skills and goals. The projects in this book are easily made, and no special tools are required. The three basic types of hand-built pottery are included—slab, coil, and pinch. For slab projects the clay is rolled to a uniform thickness, as cookie dough is rolled, then cut into whatever shapes and sizes are needed and joined together. Coil pots are made from coils rolled between the palms of the hands or on a flat surface. The coils are laid in circles, one on top of another, and joined together. Pinch pots are made by inserting a thumb into a ball of clay and then pinching the clay between the thumb on the inside and the fingers on the outside while rotating the ball of clay.

Before beginning the projects themselves, it is suggested that the potter study the section describing preparations and techniques. Each project is listed in order of difficulty under each type of pottery. Start with a simple project before going on to the more difficult ones. You can make permanent pieces of pottery from terra-cotta clay and have them fired in a kiln, or you can make the same pieces from self-hardening clay and use them for decoration *only*.

With the instructions in this book as a guide, use your imagination and ideas to make what pleases you. Later you may want to throw a pot on a potter's wheel. Whatever you decide, enjoy your adventures with pottery!

BEFORE YOU BEGIN: PREPARATION AND TECHNIQUES

Work Area. You'll need a solid table or counter to work on. Spread several layers of newspaper on it. Then place a large, heavy cloth or the rough underside of oilcloth on the surface for rolling out clay. Wear old, washable clothing. To remove clay spills from clothes, let them dry, and brush the clay out. Clean up the work area with paper towels and a damp sponge.

Clay. Two kinds of clay—terra-cotta and self-hardening —are used in this book. Both can be purchased, ready to use, in art stores and hobby shops. They are usually sold in sealed plastic bags, packaged in five-pound boxes.

Terra-cotta is a red-earthenware clay containing ground-up, prefired clay called *grog*. It is an easy clay to work with and very durable, but it must be fired in a kiln to be permanently hard. After glazing and firing, pots made of terra cotta are waterproof and can be used to hold food or liquids.

Self-hardening clay is also easy to handle and shape. It contains a self-hardening chemical drier that gives it strength after it hardens. Unlike terra-cotta containers, self-hardening clay objects cannot be fired in a kiln nor can they be used to hold food or liquids.

Clay Measurements and Dimensions. Since clays vary a little in weight, pound and ounce measurements given in this book are approximate. Additional clay has been included in the slab and coil projects to make rolling and coiling easier. For weighing clay, you will need scales that record pounds and ounces such as kitchen or baby scales. *All dimensions in this book are listed with width first.*

Wedging. The process of removing air pockets from clay is called *wedging.* All clay used for projects in this book must first be wedged. If air pockets are not removed, the pot will be uneven and lumpy, and terra-cotta pots may explode while they are being fired. An easy way to wedge clay is to throw it from a standing position twenty times onto a cloth placed on the floor.

Crosshatching. This is the process of scratching cross marks on clay at the points where two pieces of clay will be joined. A table fork makes good crosshatching marks on most pottery pieces. On smaller pieces you may want to use a toothpick or a nail to scratch the marks in the clay.

Slip. Liquid clay that is used like glue is known as slip. Before two pieces of pottery are joined, slip is brushed over the crosshatched marks. A mixture of one ounce of clay and an ounce of water is enough for any project in this book.

Paddling. This is just what it sounds like—paddling the clay gently with any flat piece of wood. A good paddle would be about two inches wide at the paddling end. You may use a flat kitchen utensil or a wooden ruler. Paddling gives shape to pottery pieces such as mugs, vases, and dishes. Paddle the area that sticks out too far, and then gently paddle all the way around until the shape is just right. Paddling will also strengthen pots that are wobbly. Any tall pot will need a lot of paddling.

Glazing and Painting. Ceramic glaze is a glassy coating painted on terra-cotta pottery before high firing. You can purchase ceramic glaze in a variety of colors at hobby shops and art stores. In addition to giving pots a colorful finish, ceramic glazes make the pottery waterproof after it is fired. Some glazes, however, are not safe to use on pottery that is meant to hold foods or liquids. Before applying glazes on these pieces, be sure the label on the bottle says it is safe. Any ceramic glaze can be used on pottery that will be solely decorative.

Water-base acrylics are used to decorate pottery pieces made from self-hardening clay. You can purchase them in art stores, hobby shops, and sometimes in variety stores. Tempera paint, found in these same places, will also give an attractive finish, but you must apply a coat of shellac or varnish over the tempera to prevent smearing. Acrylic paints come in many bright colors, and after one color has dried you may paint a design of a different color directly over it.

Firing. This is the process of baking terra-cotta pottery in a kiln, a special oven where temperatures reach above 2600°F. Since an ordinary thermometer cannot record these high temperatures, they are measured instead by special pyrometric cones. These cones, set in a pat of clay and placed in the kiln, melt down at certain definite temperatures. In this book, unglazed terra-cotta pieces are first fired at "low," cone 07, which is about 1814°F. This means that a red-clay pyrometric cone 07 placed in the kiln with the pottery will flatten out when the kiln temperature has reached 1814°F. When it does, the kiln should be turned off. When we fire at "high," about 2246°F., cone 6 is placed in the kiln with the pottery and will melt down when the temperature reaches 2246°F. High firing bakes the glaze on pottery that has already been fired at low.

Most people do not own kilns and will have to find someone to fire their pottery for them. Many colleges and some grade schools and high schools have kilns in their art departments. Community centers, churches, and even some city parks where hobby lessons are given often have a kiln. Some stores and hobby shops will fire pottery for a fee. If not, they can probably direct you to artists who have kilns in their private workshops or studios and will fire pottery at commercial rates.

Drying. Clay pots should dry slowly and be turned to different positions each day to help them dry evenly. It may take as long as a week for large pieces to dry. If tiny cracks develop while drying, brush with slip and rub smooth with your fingers.

Storage. Clay should be stored in air-tight containers such as coffee cans or plastic bags.

Scraps. Save all clay scraps in a plastic bag. If they dry out, add a little water.

Designs and Impressions. It is fun to find "stamps" with which you can make designs and impressions on your clay pots. Before you begin your project, locate several items to use as decorations. Nature is a good source. Gather seed pods, small rocks, seashells, feathers, and wood bark. Your house is another good place to look. Bolts, screws, paper clips, pencil erasers, old jewelry, buttons, lids from small bottles and from felt markers, screening, plastic berry boxes, table forks, clothespins, lace, and rickrack make interesting designs and patterns in the clay.

You may even want to make your own identifying seal to use for "signing" your pottery. Just cut out a small design from a scrap of clay about one-quarter inch thick. It can be a flower, an airplane, a worm—whatever you like. Or it might be a design of circles or your own initials. Mount it on a flat piece of clay a little larger than your design. Crosshatch the two surfaces and brush with slip. Let it dry. If you have your seal fired, it will be permanent and can be used for years.

SLAB PROJECTS

TILE

makes one tile, approximately 6 inches square

MATERIALS:

terra-cotta clay, 1 pound, 8 ounces
   (if tile is to be fired in a kiln) *or*
self-hardening clay, 1 pound, 8 ounces
   (if tile is not to be fired)
ceramic glazes, 2 or 3 colors
   (for terra-cotta clay) *or*
water-base acrylics, 2 or 3 colors
   (for self-hardening clay)
felt, 9 inches square (optional)
glue, white household, like Elmer's or Sobo (optional)

TOOLS:

kitchen scales
heavy cloth, 27 inches square
rolling pin
ruler
cardboard, 6 inches square
table knife
3 jar lids, different sizes
paper towel
damp sponge
2 paintbrushes, small flat (about $\frac{1}{2}$ inch)
   and small round (for detail)

STEPS:

1. Weigh out the amount of clay listed. Place the cloth on a hard floor. Wedge the clay by throwing it onto the cloth twenty times.

2. Move the cloth to a table. Roll out the clay ½ inch thick (Figure 1).

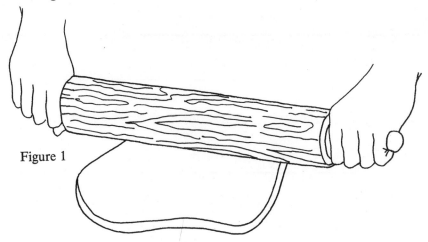

Figure 1

3. Lay the cardboard on the clay. Cut along the edges with a knife. Remove the cardboard. Save the clay scraps.

4. Using the lids, make a design of different-sized circles in the tile (Figure 2). Lift the tile, and scratch your initials on the bottom. Set on a paper towel to dry.

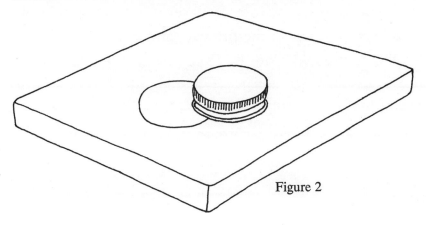

Figure 2

5. If your tile is made of self-hardening clay, paint as you wish. Let dry. Use as a hot-dish stand or as decoration.

6. If your tile is made of terra-cotta clay, first have it low fired in a kiln.

7. Wipe with a damp sponge. Paint with the glazes as you wish. Do not paint glaze on the bottom.

8. Then have your tile high fired in a kiln. Use as a hot-dish stand or as a decoration (Figure 3).

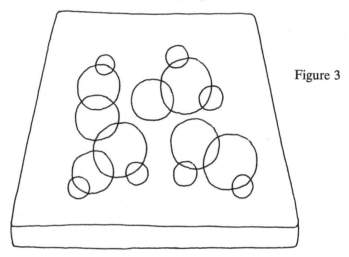

Figure 3

9. In order to prevent the back of the tile from scratching surfaces, you may want to cover it with a piece of felt. Simply cut the felt to the tile size, and cover the tile with a white-household glue. Lay the felt on the back of the tile. Place on a flat surface (felt side down), and let dry. If you cover the back with felt, you may want to scratch your initials on the top, perhaps in a lower corner.

CHRISTMAS ORNAMENTS:
BELL AND CHRISTMAS TREE

makes two ornaments

MATERIALS:

terra-cotta clay, 5 ounces

   (if ornaments are to be fired in a kiln) *or*

self-hardening clay, 5 ounces

   (if ornaments are not to be fired)

slip (½ ounce clay mixed with ½ ounce water)

ceramic glazes, 2 colors

   (for terra-cotta clay) *or*

water-base acrylics, 2 colors

   (for self-hardening clay)

2 ornament hangers or ribbon

TOOLS:

kitchen scales

heavy cloth, 27 inches square

rolling pin

ruler

metal cookie cutters, bell and Christmas-tree shapes

table knife and fork

large nail

paper towel

damp sponge

2 paintbrushes, small flat (about ½ inch)

   and small round (for detail)

STEPS:

1. Weigh out the amount of clay listed. Place the cloth on a hard floor. Wedge the clay by throwing it onto the cloth twenty times.

2. Move the cloth to a table. Roll out the clay ¼ inch thick (Figure 1).

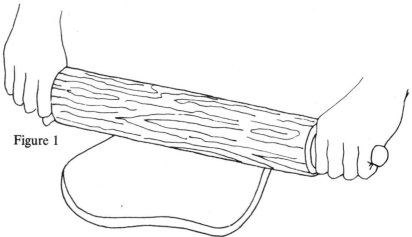

Figure 1

3. Press the cookie cutters through the clay. Remove. (Figure 2.) If clay sticks to the cutter, press out gently with your finger. Save the clay scraps.

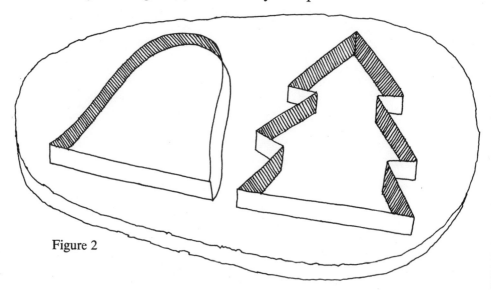

Figure 2

4. With a nail, make a hole ¼ inch from the top of the clay cookies.

5. Decorate the ornaments as you wish. To make round objects for the tree ornaments or the bell ringer, roll a small ball of clay between the palms of your hands. Cross-hatch the ball and the place it will join the cookie by scratching cross marks with a fork. Brush the marks with slip, which serves as glue, and press in place (Figure 3).

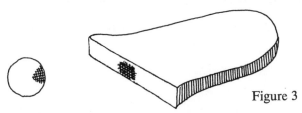

Figure 3

Make desired line decorations with a knife or fork. Scratch your initials on the back, and set right side up on a paper towel to dry.

6. If your ornaments are made of self-hardening clay, paint as you wish, and let dry. Fasten to the tree with an ornament hanger or ribbon (Figure 4).

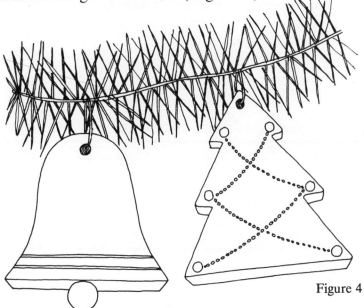

Figure 4

7. If your ornaments are made of terra-cotta clay, first have them low fired in a kiln.

8. Wipe with a damp sponge. Paint with the glazes as you wish. Do not paint glaze on the backs.

9. Then have the ornaments high fired in a kiln. Fasten to the tree with hangers or ribbon. You may want to use your ornaments to decorate Christmas packages or to hang from the mantle.

WALL MIRROR

makes one mirror, approximately 3½ inches by 5 inches

MATERIALS:

terra-cotta clay, 8 ounces
   (if mirror frame is to be fired in a kiln) *or*
self-hardening clay, 8 ounces
   (if mirror frame is not to be fired)
ceramic glazes, a dark and a light color
   (for terra-cotta clay) *or*
water-base acrylics, a dark and a light color
   (for self-hardening clay)
round mirror, 1¾ inches in diameter
   or a pocket mirror at least 1¾ inches wide
tape, masking or plastic, 12 inches
decorative cord or a leather thong, 12 inches long

TOOLS:

kitchen scales
heavy cloth, 27 inches square
rolling pin
ruler
cardboard, 3½ inches by 5 inches
table knife
jar lid, 1¼ inches in diameter
large nail
large button or heavy aluminum foil crumpled into a ball
paper towel
damp sponge
paintbrush, ½ inch wide

STEPS:

1. Weigh out the amount of clay listed. Place the cloth on a hard floor. Wedge the clay by throwing it onto the cloth twenty times.

2. Move the cloth to a table. Roll out the clay ¼ inch thick (Figure 1). Lay the cardboard on the clay. Cut

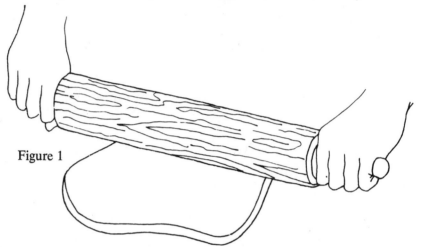

Figure 1

along the edges with a knife to make a rectangle. Remove the cardboard. Save clay scraps.

3. At least half an inch from any edge, mark a circle with the lid and cut it out with a knife (Figure 2). Near the top

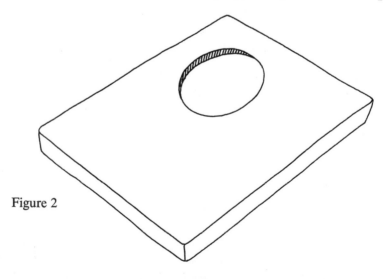

Figure 2

center of the clay, ⅜ inch from the edge, make two nail holes an inch apart (Figure 3).

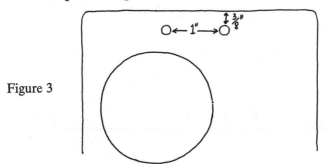

Figure 3

4. Make a design by pressing the button or foil ball into the clay, or use your own stamp (see page 11) to make impressions in the clay. Scratch your initials on the back. Set on a paper towel and let dry.

5. If your mirror frame is made of self-hardening clay, paint with the dark color. Let dry. Dip the paintbrush in the light color and wipe off most of the paint on the edge of the jar. Stroke the brush here and there as you wish on the mirror frame. Let dry.

6. Tape the mirror on the back of the frame behind the hole (Figure 4). Insert the cord or string through the nail

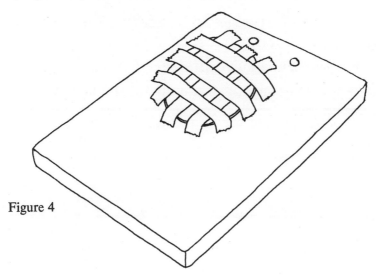

Figure 4

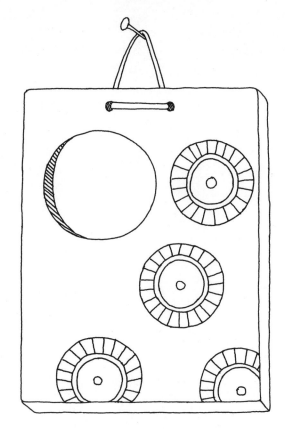

Figure 5

holes. Tie a knot. Hang mirror on the wall (Figure 5).

7. If your mirror frame is made of terra-cotta clay, first have it low fired in a kiln.

8. Wipe with a damp sponge. Paint with the dark glaze. With a sponge, wipe part of the glaze off. Paint with the light glaze. Do not paint glaze on the bottom.

9. Then have the mirror frame high fired in a kiln.

10. Attach the mirror and hang on the wall as described in Step 6.

LEAF DISH

makes a dish about 7 inches by 7 inches

MATERIALS:

terra-cotta clay, 2 pounds 8 ounces
   (if dish is to be fired in a kiln) *or*
self-hardening clay, 2 pounds 8 ounces
   (if dish is not to be fired)
slip (1 ounce clay mixed with 1 ounce water)
ceramic glazes, green and a darker color
   (for terra-cotta clay) *or*
water-base acrylics, green and a darker color
   (for self-hardening clay)

TOOLS:

kitchen scales
heavy cloth, 27 inches square
rolling pin
ruler
large leaf with stem (such as a maple or grape)
table knife and fork
pan of water
paper towels
damp sponge
2 paintbrushes, small flat (about ½ inch)
   and small round (for detail)

STEPS:

1. Weigh out the amount of clay listed. Place the cloth on a hard floor. Wedge the clay by throwing it onto the cloth twenty times.

2. Move the cloth to a table. Roll out the clay ⅜ inch thick (Figure 1). Lay the leaf on the clay right side up. Gently roll the rolling pin over the leaf several times.

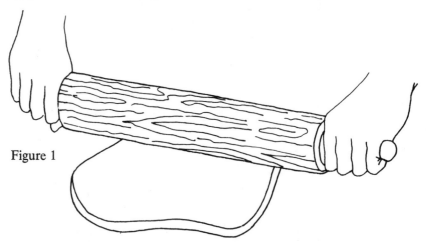

Figure 1

3. With a knife, cut around the edges of the leaf. If it has many small scallops, cut around only the larger ones. Carefully cut around the stem, leaving ¼ inch on either side. This extra width of clay will make the stem, or handle, stronger (Figure 2). Remove the leaf. Save the scraps.

4. Scratch your initials on the bottom of the leaf. Set the leaf on a table right side up, and bend up slightly the edges of the leaf and the stem. If any cracks appear, paint with slip and rub gently with your fingers. Prop up the edges with crumpled paper towels (Figure 3). Set on a paper towel, and let dry.

5. If your dish is made of self-hardening clay, paint it

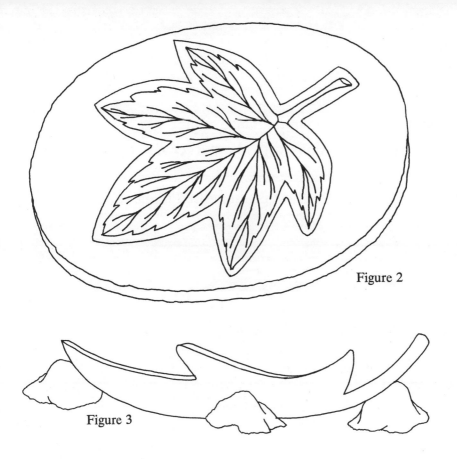

Figure 2

Figure 3

green, and then paint the veins with the darker color. Let dry and use as a decoration only (Figure 4). Do not put food or liquids in the dish.

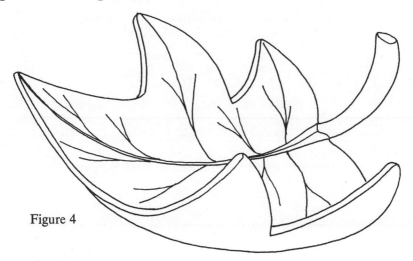

Figure 4

6. If your dish is made of terra-cotta clay, first have it low fired in a kiln.

7. Wipe with a damp sponge. Paint the dish green, and then paint the veins with the darker color. Do not paint glaze on the bottom.

8. Then have the leaf dish high fired in a kiln. Use to hold food or candy, as any other dish.

BOX WITH LID

makes a box approximately 4 inches by 6 inches

MATERIALS:

terra-cotta clay, 3 pounds
   (if box is to be fired in a kiln) *or*
self-hardening clay, 3 pounds
   (if box is not to be fired)
slip (1 ounce clay mixed with 1 ounce water)
ceramic glazes, 2 or 3 colors
   (for terra-cotta clay) *or*
water-base acrylics, 2 or 3 colors
   (for self-hardening clay)

TOOLS:

kitchen scales
cardboard, 7 inches by 9 inches
cardboard, 4 inches by 5¾ inches
pencil
ruler
scissors
heavy cloth, 27 inches square
rolling pin
table knife and fork
pan of water
paper towel
damp sponge
bowl or large glass
paintbrush, ½ inch wide

BOX

1. Weigh out the amount of clay listed. Lay the larger cardboard on a table. Measure and draw a line across the cardboard two inches from the top. Draw another line two inches from the bottom and a line two inches from each side. Cut out the corners along the lines, and discard them (Figure 1).

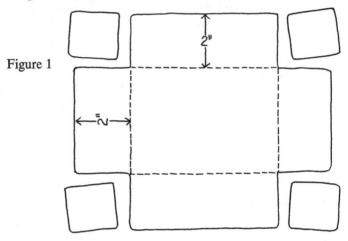

Figure 1

2"

2"

2. Place the cloth on a hard floor. Wedge the clay by throwing it onto the cloth twenty times.

3. Move the cloth to a table. Roll out the clay ⅜ inch thick (Figure 2).

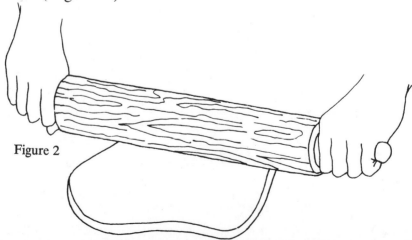

Figure 2

4. Lay the cardboard on the clay, and cut along the edges with a knife. Remove cardboard.

5. From the remaining clay, roll out a three-ounce ball between the palms of your hands until it is sausage-shaped. Then roll it back and forth on the cloth to make a ⅜-inch coil (Figure 3). Dip your hands in water occasionally to keep them moist. Cut the coil into four equal pieces, and set aside.

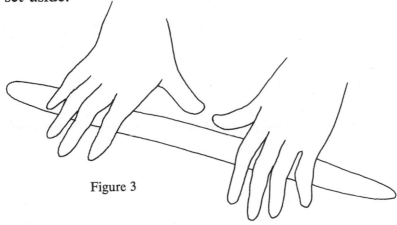

Figure 3

6. Bend up one side and one end of the box. If tiny cracks appear in the clay, moisten them with slip and rub lightly with your fingers. Crosshatch the edges to be joined by scratching the clay with a fork (Figure 4). Brush these

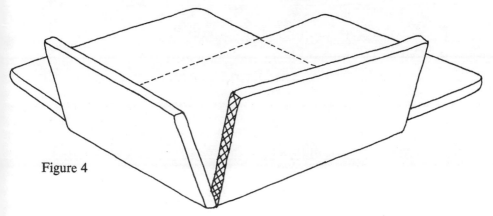

Figure 4

marks with slip, which serves as glue, and press the corners together. Bend the other side and the other end of the box, and fasten the corners together using the same methods. Then join the two remaining corners in the same way.
7. Take one of the four coils, and crosshatch one side. Paint with slip, and press vertically against the inside of one corner (Figure 5). Work it in with your fingers until

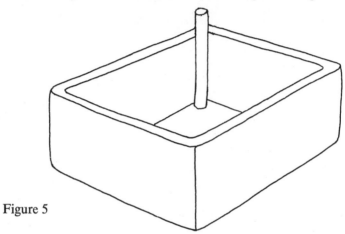

Figure 5

it is smooth, keeping one hand outside the corner as you work. Cut off the excess coil at the top. Do the same thing with the other three corners. Scratch your initials on the bottom of the box. Set upright on a paper towel, and let dry.

LID

8. Reroll the remaining clay ⅜ inch thick.
9. Cut a 1½-inch hole in the center of the smaller cardboard. Discard. Lay the cardboard on the clay, and cut around it along the edges. Do not cut out the center.
10. Roll four ounces of the unused clay into a ⅜-inch coil as in Step 5. Crosshatch one side, and paint with slip.

11. Scratch a continuous line on the underside of the lid, ¾ inch from the outside edges. Crosshatch and paint the line with slip. Press the coil into the clay along this line. Cut off both ends of the coil where they meet. Crosshatch both ends (Figure 6), brush with slip, and pressing with your fingers, work into a smooth, tight joint. Turn the lid over.

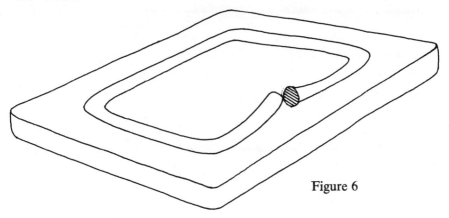

Figure 6

12. Roll a ¾-inch ball of clay. Crosshatch one side of the ball, and using the cut-out hole in the cardboard as a guide, crosshatch the center of the lid. Paint the marks with slip, and press the ball onto the lid.

13. Lay the lid upside down on the cardboard, with the ball extending down through the cut-out hole. Set the cardboard on a bowl or a large glass, and let the lid dry (Figure 7).

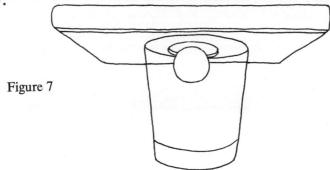

Figure 7

14. If your box is made of self-hardening clay, paint it inside and out as you wish. You might wish to paint flowers or a design on it in another color. Set on a paper towel, and let dry.

15. If your box is made of terra-cotta clay, first have it low fired in a kiln.

16. Wipe with a damp sponge. Paint the glazes inside and out as you wish. Do not paint glaze on the bottom.

17. Then have the box high fired in a kiln. Your box will make an attractive jewel box or a handy container for stamps, buttons, or other small objects (Figure 8).

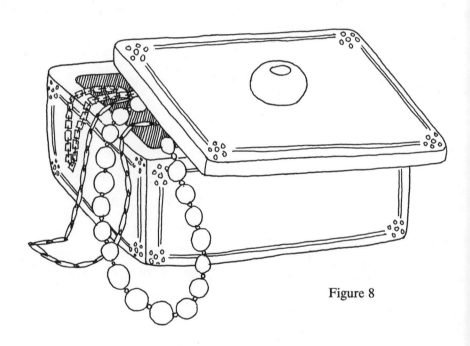

Figure 8

COIL PROJECTS

BEAD

makes one bead

MATERIALS:

terra-cotta clay, ⅓ ounce
   (if bead is to be fired in a kiln) *or*
self-hardening clay, ⅓ ounce
   (if bead is not to be fired)
ceramic glazes, 1 or 2 colors
   (for terra-cotta clay) *or*
water-base acrylics, 1 or 2 colors
   (for self-hardening clay)
material to string bead
   (such as pretty string, nylon macramé cord,
   or a leather thong), about 24 inches

TOOLS:

kitchen scales
heavy cloth, 27 inches square
large nail
paper towel
damp sponge
paintbrush, small, round

STEPS:

1. Weigh out the amount of clay listed. Place the cloth on a hard floor. Wedge the clay by throwing it onto the cloth twenty times.

2. Roll the clay into a ball between the palms of your hands. Leave it round if you wish, or roll it into a sausage shape. If you want, scratch a design on the bead with the nail. If your bead is made of self-hardening clay, you may want to decorate it with a small feather or pretty glitter. (Figure 1).

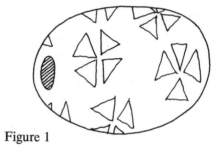

Figure 1

3. Push the nail through the center of the bead to make a hole. Set on a paper towel to dry.

4. If the bead is made of self-hardening clay, paint as you wish. Let dry, and string on a cord to make a necklace (Figure 2).

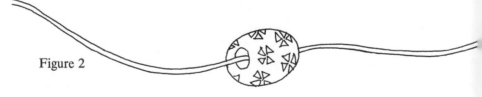

Figure 2

5. If the bead is made of terra-cotta clay, have it first low fired in a kiln.

34 Coil Projects

6. Wipe with a damp sponge. Paint with the glazes as you wish. Let dry.

7. Then have the bead high fired in a kiln. String on a colorful cord or whatever you choose.

8. If you want, make several beads. Some may be round, others sausage-shaped. String them together (Figure 3).

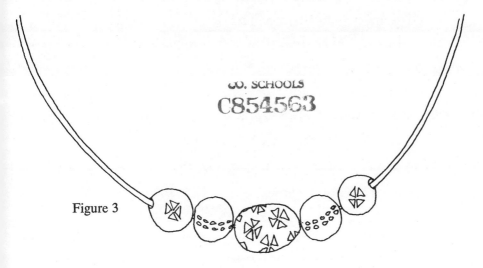

Figure 3

HANGING PLANTER

makes a planter 4 inches by 3 inches

MATERIALS:
terra-cotta clay, 2 pounds
  (if planter is to be fired in a kiln) *or*
self-hardening clay, 2 pounds
  (if planter is not to be fired)
slip (1 ounce clay mixed with 1 ounce water)
ceramic glaze, any color
  (for terra-cotta clay) *or*
water-base acrylic, any color
  (for self-hardening clay)
heavy cord, 2 yards

TOOLS:
kitchen scales
heavy cloth, 27 inches square
rolling pin
ruler
glass or can, 3 inches in diameter
table knife and fork
large nail
pan of water
paper towel
damp sponge
paintbrush, ½ inch wide

STEPS:

1. Weigh out the amount of clay listed. Place the cloth on a hard floor. Wedge the clay by throwing it onto the cloth twenty times.

2. Move the cloth to a table. Roll out six ounces of the clay ½ inch thick (Figure 1). Mark a circle with the glass

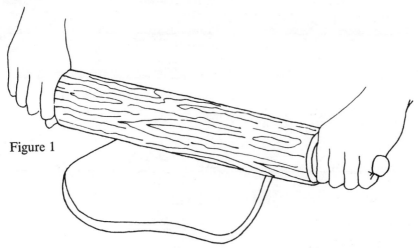

Figure 1

and cut out with a knife. The circle of clay will be the base of the planter. Save the clay scraps.

3. Cut the remaining clay into seven equal pieces. Roll each piece between the palms of your hands until it is sausage-shaped. Then roll it back and forth on the cloth to make a ½-inch coil (Figure 2). Dip your hands in water occasionally to keep them moist.

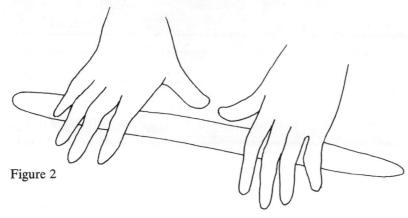

Figure 2

4. Crosshatch the outer edge of the base and one side of a coil by scratching cross marks with a fork. Brush the marks with slip, which serves as glue. Lay the coil around the edge of the base with the crosshatching against the base. Cut off both ends of the coil where they meet. Crosshatch the ends (Figure 3), and brush with slip. Press

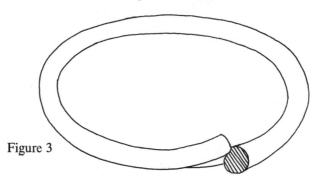

Figure 3

the ends together, and work the clay with your fingers until the joint is tight and smooth. Press the coil to the base. Blend the joint with your fingers until it is even.

5. Place another coil exactly on top of the first. Cut and join the ends as described in Step 4. Let the ends meet at another part of the planter. Crosshatch and paint with slip where the two coils touch. Smooth the coil down on the inside with your fingers while supporting the outside with your other hand (Figure 4). Put the other five coils on the same way. Make sure that the ends of each coil join together at a different place. Continue to smooth the coils down on the inside with your fingers, but let the coil shapes show on the outside.

6. With a nail make three holes, equal distances apart, through the second coil from the top. Scratch your initials

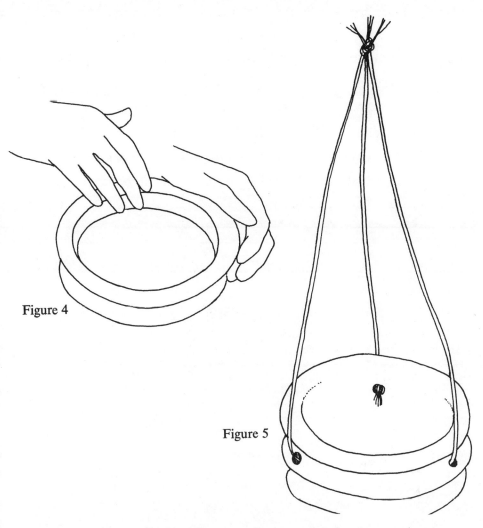

Figure 4

Figure 5

on the bottom of the planter. Set it upright on a paper towel. Let dry.

7. If your planter is made of self-hardening clay, paint it inside and out. Let dry.

8. Divide and cut the cord into thirds. Tie a large knot in each cord. Put one cord through each hole with the knot on the inside of the planter. Tie the cords together at the top (Figure 5). Use for artificial plant. Do not put soil or water in the planter.

9. If your planter is made of terra-cotta clay, first have it low fired in a kiln.

10. Wipe with a damp sponge. Paint the glaze inside and out. Do not paint glaze on the bottom.

11. Then have your planter high fired in a kiln. Attach the cord as in Step 8. Fill with dirt and whatever plant you choose (Figure 6).

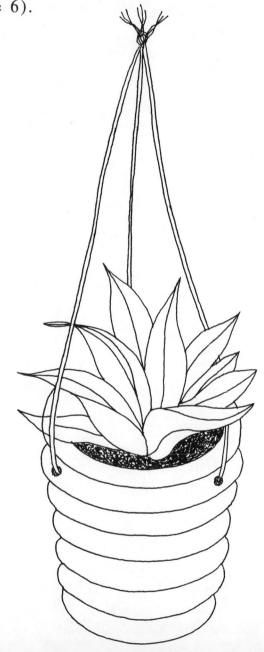

Figure 6

COIL VASE

makes a vase 4 inches by 4 inches

MATERIALS:

terra-cotta clay, 2 pounds
   (if vase is to be fired in a kiln *or*
self-hardening clay, 2 pounds
   (if vase is not to be fired)
slip (1 ounce clay mixed with 1 ounce water)
ceramic glaze, any color
   (for terra-cotta clay) *or*
water-base acrylic, any color
   (for self-hardening clay)

TOOLS:

kitchen scales
heavy cloth, 27 inches square
rolling pin
ruler
glass or can, $1\frac{1}{2}$ inches in diameter
table knife and fork
pan of water
paper towel
damp sponge
paintbrush, $\frac{1}{2}$ inch wide

STEPS:

1. Weigh out the amount of clay listed. Place the cloth on a hard floor. Wedge the clay by throwing it onto the cloth twenty times.

2. Move the cloth to a table. Roll out 1½ ounces of clay ½ inch thick (Figure 1). Mark a circle with the rim of

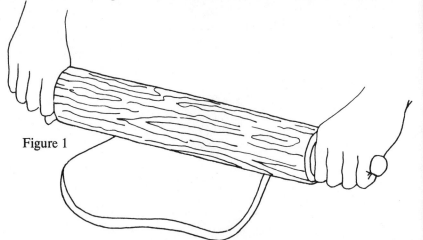

Figure 1

the glass, and cut it out with a knife. The circle of clay will be the base of the vase. Save the clay scraps.

3. From the remaining clay, cut out three 3½-ounce pieces and six 3-ounce pieces. You will have three long coils and six shorter ones. Roll each piece between the palms of your hands until it is sausage-shaped. Then roll it back and forth on the cloth to make a ½-inch coil (Figure 2).

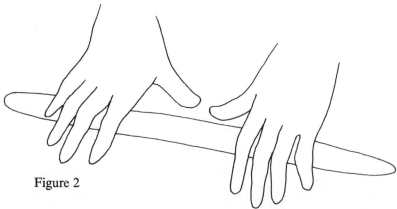

Figure 2

Dip your hands in water occasionally to keep them moist.
4. Crosshatch the outer edge of the base and one side of a *short coil* by scratching cross marks with a fork. Brush the marks with slip, which serves as glue. Lay the short coil around the edge of the base with the crosshatching against the base. Cut off both ends of the coil where

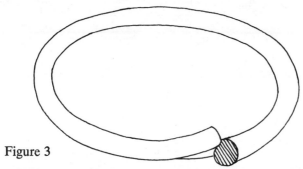

Figure 3

they meet. Crosshatch both ends (Figure 3), and brush with slip. Press the ends together, and work the clay with your fingers until the joint is smooth and tight. Press the coil to the base. Blend the joint with your fingers until it is even.
5. Place another *short coil* on top of the first one, but position it so that the *inside* edge is in line with the center of the first coil, and the outside edge extends out beyond the first coil (Figure 4). Let the ends meet in a different part

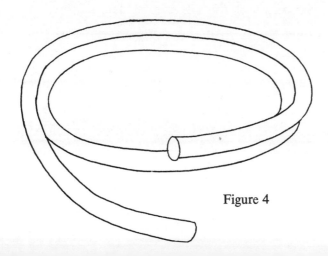

Figure 4

of the vase. Cut off both ends of the coil where they meet. Crosshatch and paint with slip where the two coils touch. Smooth the coil down into the vase on the inside with your fingers while supporting the outside with your other hand (Figure 5). Put the next three coils on the same way. First

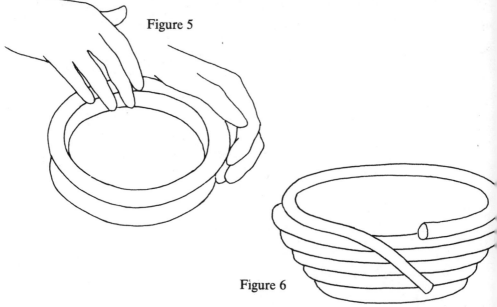

Figure 5

Figure 6

use a *short coil,* then two of the *long coils.* Continue to position the coils so that the *outside edges* extend beyond the previous coil.

6. Then add a long coil, but this time place the *outside* edge even with the center of the previous coil (Figure 6). Add three more of the *short coils* the same way, continuing to place them with the outside edges in line with the center of the previous coil. Scratch your initials on the bottom of the vase. Set upright on a paper towel to dry.

7. If your vase is made of self-hardening clay, paint it as you wish. Let it dry, and use it as a decoration or to hold

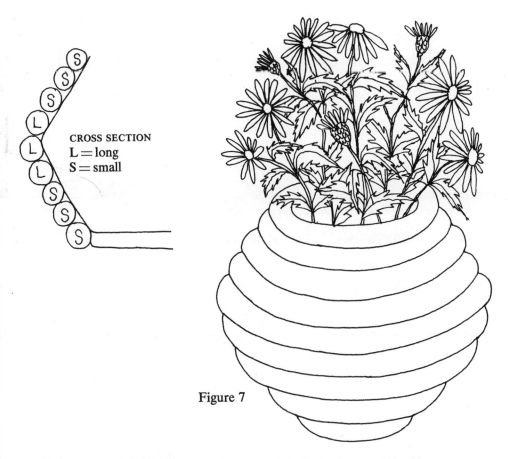

CROSS SECTION
L = long
S = small

Figure 7

artificial or dried flowers (Figure 7). Do not put water in the vase.

8. If your vase is made of terra-cotta clay, first have it low fired in a kiln.

9. Wipe the inside and outside of the vase with a damp sponge. Pour a ceramic glaze in the vase, rotating it until the inside is evenly coated. Pour any leftover glaze back into the jar. Paint the glaze on the outside. Do not paint glaze on the bottom.

10. Then have your vase high fired in a kiln. Fill with dirt or water to hold live flowers or plants.

MUG

makes a mug about 2 inches in diameter

MATERIALS:

terra-cotta clay, 1 pound 8 ounces
   (if mug is to be fired in a kiln) *or*
self-hardening clay, 1 pound 8 ounces
   (if mug is not to be fired)
slip (1 ounce clay mixed with 1 ounce water)
ceramic glazes, safe for food or drink, any two colors
   (for terra-cotta clay) *or*
water-base acrylics, any two colors
   (for self-hardening clay)

TOOLS:

kitchen scales
heavy cloth, 27 inches square
rolling pin
ruler
glass or can, 2 inches in diameter
table knife and fork
pan of water
paper towel
damp sponge
flat wooden paddle or ruler
twine, 4 yards or 24 rubber bands
paintbrush, ½ inch wide

STEPS:

1. Weigh out the amount of clay listed. Place the cloth on a hard floor. Wedge the clay by throwing it onto the cloth twenty times.

2. Move the cloth to a table. Roll out four ounces of the clay ⅜ inch thick.

3. Mark a circle with the rim of a glass, and cut it out with a knife. The circle of clay will be the base of the mug. Save the scraps.

4. Cut the remaining clay into eleven equal pieces. Roll each piece between the palms of your hands until it is sausage-shaped. Then roll it back and forth on the cloth to make a ⅜-inch coil (Figure 1). Dip your hands in water occasionally to keep them moist.

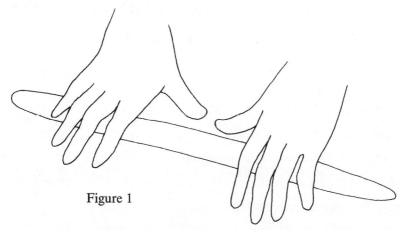

Figure 1

5. Crosshatch the outer edge of the base and one side of a coil by scratching cross marks with a fork. Brush the marks with slip, which serves as glue. Lay the coil around the edge of the base with the crosshatching against the base. Cut off both ends of the coil where they meet.

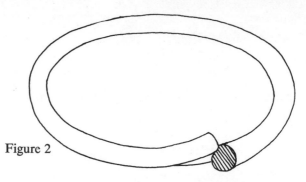

Figure 2

Crosshatch both ends (Figure 2), and brush with slip. Press the ends together, and work the clay with your fingers until the joint is smooth and tight. Press the coil to the base. Blend the joint until it is even.

6. Put another coil exactly on top of the first, but let the ends meet in a different part of the mug. Crosshatch and paint with slip where the two coils touch. Smooth the coil down into the mug on the inside with your fingers while supporting the outside with your other hand (Figure 3). Put nine more coils on the same way. Smooth the outside surface of the mug as you did the inside, keeping your hands moist.

7. Form a design by winding twine or pressing rubber bands into the outside surface of the mug. Set the mug on a table, and place one hand inside. With the other hand paddle gently with a wooden ruler or paddle, turning the mug slowly to cover the entire surface (Figure 4). Remove twine or rubber bands. If necessary, carefully reshape the mug with your hands.

8. Crosshatch a strip ½ inch wide and 1½ inches long at the top of the mug and directly below at the bottom of the mug. Paint with slip. Crosshatch and paint with slip 1½ inches of one end of the coil. Starting 1½ inches from

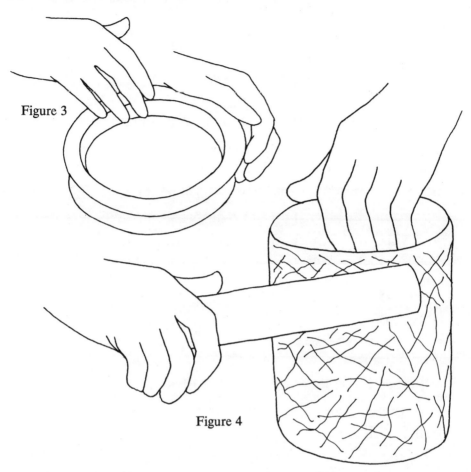

Figure 3

Figure 4

the top of the mug, press the crosshatching on the coil to the crosshatching on the mug, holding the remainder of the coil above the mug. Carefully bend the coil downward to form the handle, leaving plenty of finger room in the handle loop (Figure 5). If the handle seems too long, cut

Figure 5

off the excess. Crosshatch the bottom 1½ inches of the inside handle and paint with slip. Press and work into the mug (Figure 6). Check the handle for cracks. If they occur, brush them with slip and work them smooth with your fingers. Scratch your initials on the bottom of the mug. Set upright on a paper towel. Let dry.

9. If your mug is made of self-hardening clay, paint with one color. Let dry. Dip the paintbrush in the other color and wipe most of the paint off on the edges of the jar. Stroke the brush here and there as you wish on the mug. Let it dry and use as a decoration. Do not put liquids in it.

10. If your mug is made of terra-cotta clay, first have it low fired in a kiln.

11. Wipe with a damp sponge. Paint the inside of the mug with the glazes. Paint the outside with a dark glaze. Sponge part of the paint off. Paint the entire outside with the lighter color. Do not paint glaze on the bottom.

12. Then have the mug high fired in a kiln. Use to hold liquids, as any other mug.

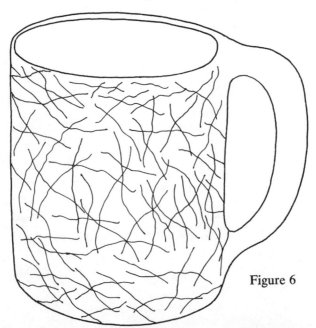

Figure 6

PINCH PROJECTS

PINCH-POT CANDLE HOLDER
makes a candle holder 3 inches high

MATERIALS:

terra-cotta clay, 8 ounces
  (if pinch-pot candle holder is to be fired in a kiln) *or*
self-hardening clay, 8 ounces
  (if pinch-pot candle holder is not to be fired)
slip (½ ounce clay mixed with ½ ounce water)
ceramic glaze, any color
  (for terra-cotta clay) *or*
water-base acrylic, any color
  (for self-hardening clay)

TOOLS:

kitchen scales
heavy cloth, 27 inches square
table fork
paper towel
damp sponge
paintbrush, ½ inch wide

STEPS:

1. Weigh out the amount of clay listed. Place the cloth on a hard floor. Wedge the clay by throwing it onto the cloth twenty times.

2. Move the cloth to a table. Divide the clay into nine equal parts. Roll each part into a smooth ball between your palms.

3. Holding a ball in one hand, push one finger of the other hand into the center of the ball. With your finger on the inside and your thumb on the outside, pinch gently until the opening is barely larger than your finger (Figure 1). Set aside.

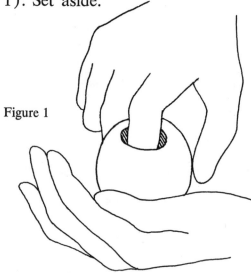

Figure 1

4. Make eight more pinch pots the same way.

5. Set five of the pots in a circle, touching each other. Position each pot so that all holes are turned outward at the same angle (Figure 2). Mark the places where they touch. Crosshatch these places by scratching cross marks with a fork (Figure 3). Brush slip on the cross marks

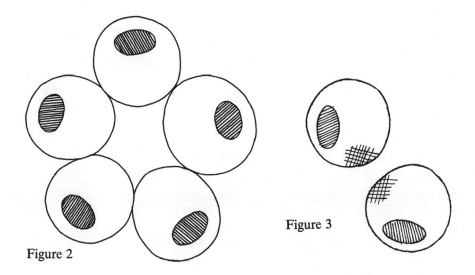

Figure 3

Figure 2

and press the pots carefully together. Set on a paper towel to dry partly.

6. Set three more pots in a circle, following the instructions given in Step 5 (Figure 4).

7. In two or three hours, carefully set the three pots on the circle of five. Mark the places where they touch. Crosshatch these places, paint with slip, and press gently together (Figure 5).

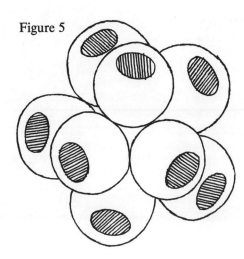

Figure 5

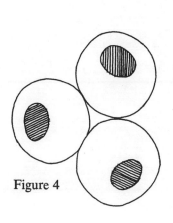

Figure 4

8. Set the remaining pot in the center of the circle of three with the opening straight up. Mark the places where they touch. Crosshatch, paint with slip, and press together as before. Scratch your initials on the bottom. Set on a paper towel to dry.

9. If your pinch-pot candle holder is made of self-hardening clay, paint inside and out and let it dry. Insert candles in the pots (Figure 6).

10. If your pinch-pot candle holder is made of terra-cotta clay, first have it low fired in a kiln.

11. Wipe inside and out with a damp sponge. Paint the glaze inside and out. Do not paint glaze on the bottom.

12. Then have it high fired in a kiln. Insert candles in the pots.

Figure 6

BAG-OF-GOLD BANK

makes a bank 4 inches in diameter

MATERIALS:

terra-cotta clay, 12 ounces
   (if bank is to be fired in a kiln) *or*
self-hardening clay, 12 ounces
   (if bank is not to be fired)
slip (1 ounce clay mixed with 1 ounce water)
ceramic glazes, a dark and a light color
   (for terra-cotta clay) *or*
water-base acrylics, a dark and a light color
   (for self-hardening clay)
rubber stopper, 1½ inches in diameter

TOOLS:

kitchen scales
heavy cloth, 27 inches square
ruler
table fork
paper towel
damp sponge
2 paintbrushes, small flat (about ½ inch)
   and small round (for detail)

STEPS:

1. Weigh out the amount of clay listed. Place the cloth on a hard floor. Wedge the clay by throwing it onto the cloth twenty times.

2. Move the cloth to a table. Set aside one ounce of clay. Roll the remaining clay into a smooth ball between your palms.

3. Holding the ball in one hand, push the thumb of the other hand into the center of the ball. Even the clay all around by pinching between your thumb on the inside and your fingers on the outside (Figure 1). Try to make the clay about $3/8$ inch thick all around.

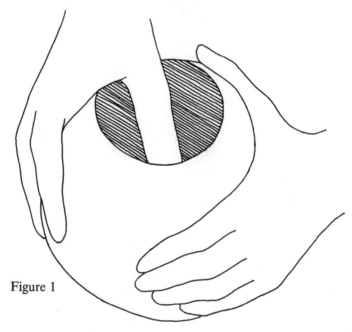

Figure 1

4. Half an inch from the top, pinch all the way around to make the clay thinner, but leave the top $3/8$ inch thick. Set on a table. Gently squeeze the clay toward the center

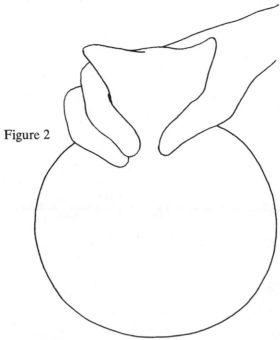

Figure 2

at the thin part (Figure 2). As you do so, the clay will wrinkle and tiny cracks may appear. Paint any cracks with slip, and smooth them with your fingers before you squeeze more. Do not squeeze completely shut. Leave a coin opening about ¼ inch by 1 inch. Smooth the opening with the handle of the table fork. Mold the top of the bag out slightly with your fingers, and leave it uneven (Figure 3). Set on a paper towel to dry for two or three hours.

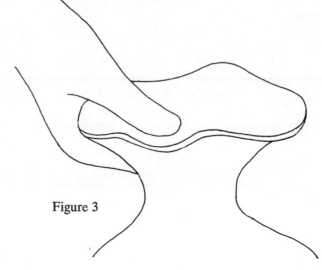

Figure 3

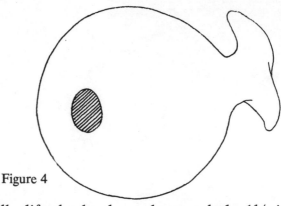

Figure 4

5. Carefully lift the bank, and cut a hole 1½ inches in diameter in the center of the bottom (Figure 4). Insert one finger, and gently press the sides of the bag out a little. Scratch your initials on the bottom.

6. Roll the remaining ounce of clay into a ⅜-inch coil (Figure 5). Put it gently around the squeezed part of the

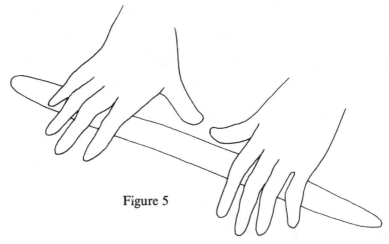

Figure 5

bag, and cross it. Mark the places where it touches. Cross-hatch these places by scratching cross marks with a fork (Figure 6). Brush with slip, which serves as glue, and press together carefully. Set on a paper towel to dry.

7. If your bank is made of self-hardening clay, paint the

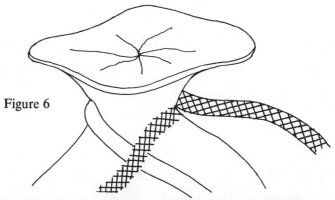

Figure 6

bag with a light color and the creases with a dark color. Let dry (Figure 7). Insert the stopper in the bottom.

8. If your bank is made of terra-cotta clay, first have it low fired in a kiln.

9. Wipe with a damp sponge. Paint the creases with a dark glaze and the entire bag a lighter color. Do not paint glaze on the bottom.

10. Then have it high fired in a kiln. Insert the stopper in the bottom.

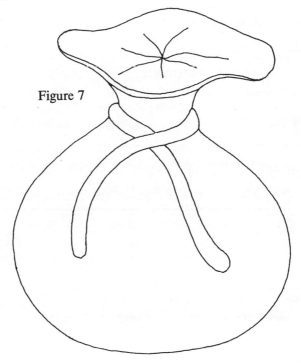

Figure 7

MUSHROOM SALT AND PEPPER SHAKERS

makes two shakers 2 inches tall

MATERIALS:

terra-cotta clay, 9 ounces
   (if shakers are to be fired in a kiln *or*
self-hardening clay, 9 ounces
   (if shakers are not to be fired)
slip (½ ounce clay mixed with ½ ounce water)
ceramic glazes, a light and a dark color
   (for terra-cotta clay) *or*
water-base acrylics, a light and a dark color
   (for self-hardening clay)
2 corks, ⅜ inch diameter

TOOLS:

kitchen scales
heavy cloth, 27 inches square
ruler
table fork
large nail
paper towel
damp sponge
2 paintbrushes, small flat (about ½ inch)
   and small round (for detail)

STEPS:

1. Weigh out the amount of clay listed. Place the cloth on a hard floor. Wedge the clay by throwing it onto the cloth twenty times.

2. Move the cloth to a table. Divide the clay in half to make two shakers. Roll out three ounces of one piece into a smooth ball between your palms.

3. Holding the ball in your left hand, push your right thumb into the center, moving the clay upward to hollow out the ball (Figure 1). Use your fingers on the outside

Figure 1

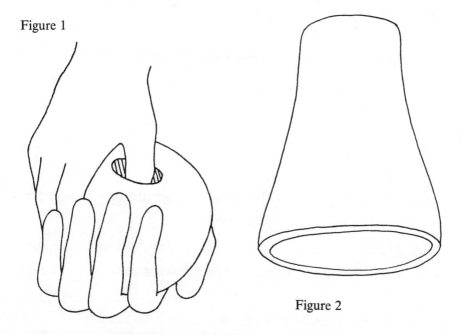

Figure 2

to pinch and shape the ball into a cylinder that is wider at the bottom (Figure 2). Push your thumb through the center of the cylinder, allowing it to come out the top. This piece will be the stem of the mushroom and should be 2¼ inches to 2¾ inches high. Working at the bottom edge, mold the edges toward the center, leaving a ⅜-inch opening for the cork (Figure 3).

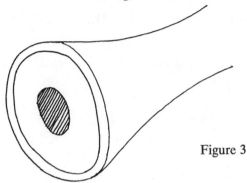

Figure 3

4. Roll the remaining 1½ ounces of the clay into a smooth ball between your palms, and pat it to make a fairly round cake about ¼ inch thick. This piece will be the cap of the mushroom. With a nail, make three holes near the center for pouring. On the underside of the cap, scratch marks extending from the center to the outside (Figure 4).

5. Set the cap carefully on the stem, making certain the holes are in the right place for the salt and pepper to come out. Lift off the cap. Crosshatch the top of the stem and the part of the cap that will touch the stem by scratch-

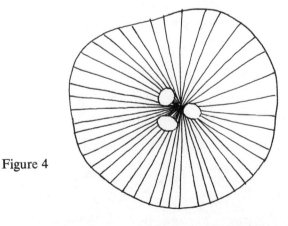

Figure 4

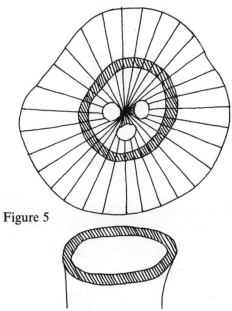

Figure 5

ing cross marks with a fork (Figure 5). Paint the marks with slip, and carefully press together. Pinch the edges of the cap down a little (Figure 6). Scratch your initials on the bottom, and set upright on a paper towel to dry.

6. Make another shaker in the same way with the remaining $4\frac{1}{2}$-ounce piece of clay. If you like, use the nail to scratch S and P on the shakers.

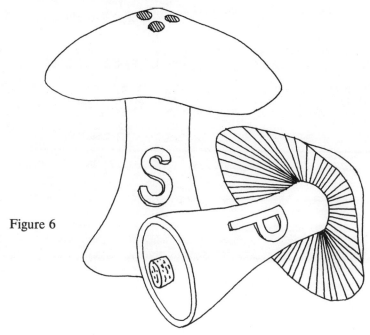

Figure 6

7. If your shakers are made of self-hardening clay, paint the underparts of the caps a dark color and the rest of the mushrooms a lighter color. Trim the corks to fit the holes.

8. If your shakers are made of terra-cotta clay, first have them low fired in a kiln.

9. Wipe with a damp sponge. Paint the underparts of the caps with a dark glaze and the rest of the mushrooms with a lighter one. Do not paint glaze on the bottoms.

10. Have the mushrooms high fired in a kiln. Trim the corks to fit the holes.

Instead of making two shakers, you may want to use all nine ounces of the clay to make one large mushroom shaker. Divide clay into two pieces, one 6-ounce piece for the stem and one 3-ounce piece for the cap. Follow the steps above. Fill with confectioners' sugar or a mixture of cinnamon and sugar to sprinkle on toast and cereal.